I Know Someone with
ADHD

Elizabeth Raum

Raintree

www.raintreepublishers.co.uk
Visit our website to find out more information about Raintree books.

To order:
☎ Phone 0845 6044371
🖨 Fax +44 (0) 1865 312263
💻 Email myorders@raintreepublishers.co.uk

Customers from outside the UK please telephone +44 1865 312262

Raintree is an imprint of Capstone Global Library Limited, a company incorporated in England and Wales having its registered office at 7 Pilgrim Street, London, EC4V 6LB – Registered company number: 6695582

Edited by Rebecca Rissman, Daniel Nunn and Siân Smith
Designed by Joanna Hinton Malivoire
Picture research by Mica Brancic
Originated by Capstone Global Library
Printed and bound in China by Leo Paper Products Ltd

ISBN 978 1 406 22071 1
15 14 13 12 11
10 9 8 7 6 5 4 3 2 1

British Library Cataloguing in Publication Data
Raum, Elizabeth.
I know someone with ADHD. – (Understanding health issues)
1. Attention-deficit hyperactivity disorder–Juvenile literature.
I. Title II. Series
616.8'589-dc22

Acknowledgements
We would like to thank the following for permission to reproduce photographs: Corbis pp. 4 (Fancy/© Deborah Jaffe), 14 (© Klaus Tiedge), 27 (© STAFF/ Reuters); Getty Images pp. 6 (Blend Images/JGI/Jamie Grill), 9 (BLOOM image), 11 (Iconica/Peter Cade), 13 (The Image Bank/LWA), 17 (Digital Vision/Supernova), 18 (Dorling Kindersley/Steve Gorton), 19 (Riser/LWA), 20 (Photodisc/Sandy Jones), 21 (Photographer's Choice/Victoria Blackie), 23 (OJO Images/Anthony Lee), 24 (Photographer's Choice/Jeff Cadge), 25 (Stone/Michael Goldman), 26 (Bloomberg/Natalie Behring), 28 (The Image Bank/John Kelly); Photolibrary pp. 12 (Cultura/Monty Rakusen), 15 (Stockbroker/ Monkey Business Images Ltd), 22 (Cusp/LWA-Dann Tardif); Shutterstock pp. 5 (© Supri Suharjoto), 10 (© Suzanne Tucker).

Cover photograph of a boy painting reproduced with permission of Corbis (© Edith Held).

We would like to thank Matthew Siegel, Ashley Wolinski, and Professor Paul Cooper for their invaluable help in the preparation of this book.

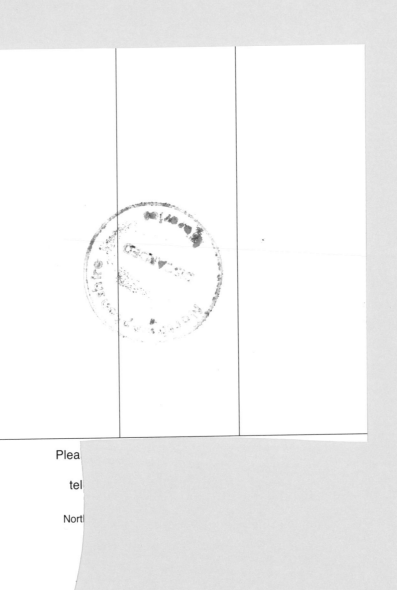

Plea

tel

Nort

Contents

Some words are printed in bold, **like this**. You can find out what they mean in the glossary.

Do you know anyone with ADHD?

Do you have a friend who has trouble paying attention? Does your friend shout out answers before the teacher finishes asking questions? Does your friend find it hard to sit still?

You cannot tell whether someone has ADHD by looking at them.

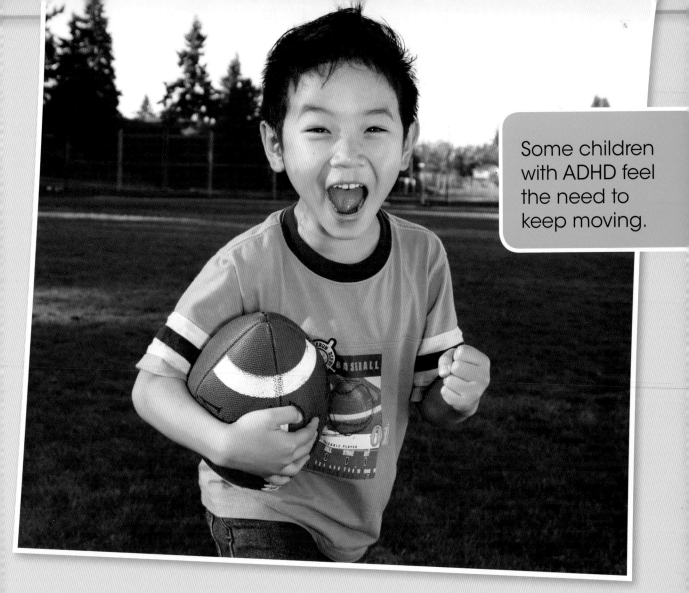

Some children with ADHD feel the need to keep moving.

If so, your friend may have ADHD. Children with ADHD may have trouble **concentrating**, sitting still, or waiting patiently.

What is ADHD?

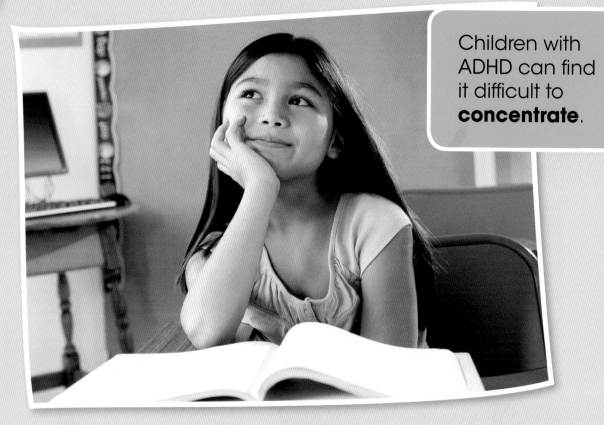

Children with ADHD can find it difficult to **concentrate**.

ADHD is a word used by doctors, teachers, and parents. ADHD stands for Attention-Deficit/Hyperactivity Disorder. This describes the different types of **behaviour** that people with ADHD might show.

Some people with ADHD can find it hard to pay attention. They might find it difficult to think about one thing for a long time. They may jump from idea to idea or from one job to another.

Children with ADHD may:

- be forgetful
- be easily **distracted**
- have trouble completing tasks
- find it difficult to listen.

Children with ADHD can also be **impulsive**. Being impulsive means doing things suddenly without thinking about what might happen.

Children with ADHD may:
- interrupt others
- say things without thinking
- find it difficult to wait for their turn
- blurt out answers before the teacher has finished asking the question.

It can be hard for some children with ADHD to wait until the teacher calls on them.

Children with ADHD are not trying to cause trouble when they act without thinking ahead. It is more difficult for them to control impulsive **behaviour** than it is for people without ADHD.

People with ADHD may also be **hyperactive**. Hyperactive people have a lot of energy. They find it difficult to sit still or be quiet for long periods of time.

Children with ADHD may sometimes:
- talk non-stop
- **fidget** or move all the time.

Resting quietly is difficult for hyperactive children.

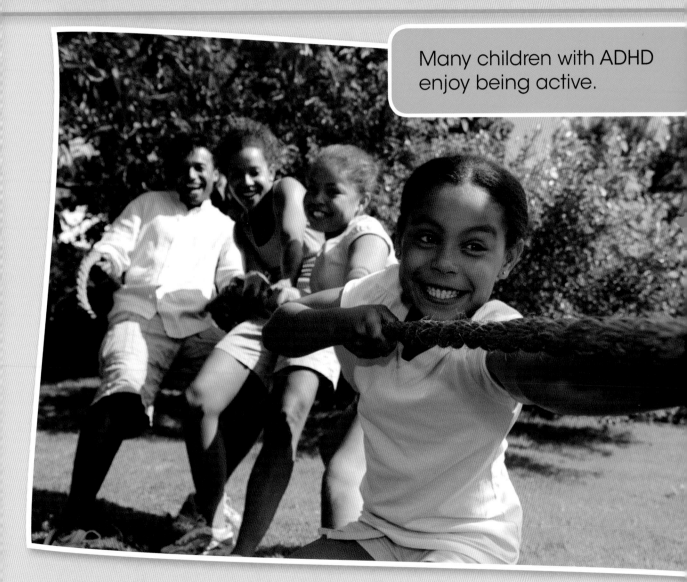

Many children with ADHD enjoy being active.

Everyone acts in these ways sometimes. When someone has ADHD though, they show some or all of these **behaviours** a lot of the time.

Causes of ADHD

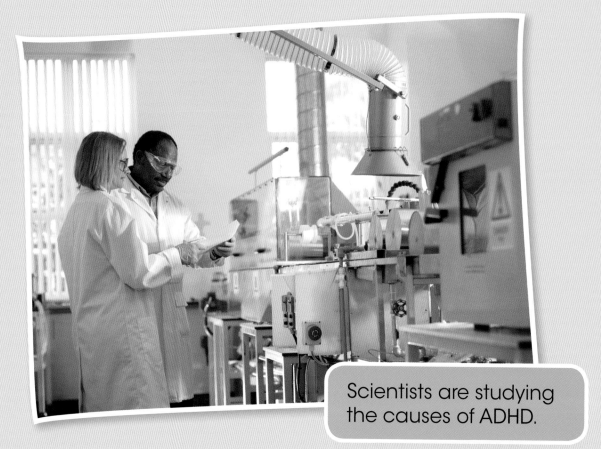

Scientists are studying the causes of ADHD.

Doctors do not know for certain what causes ADHD. But they do know that ADHD is not something you can catch like a cold. People with ADHD are as healthy as anyone else.

ADHD sometimes seems to run in families, a bit like having brown eyes or blonde hair. This means that certain people can be more likely to get ADHD. Scientists are investigating whether **chemicals** in the world around us can cause ADHD, too.

Some children with ADHD have a relative, often a parent, who also has ADHD.

Experts decide

There is no one test for ADHD. Sometimes a child realizes that something is wrong and tells a parent or teacher. Sometimes the parent or teacher might notice the signs of ADHD.

One of the best things you can do when you are worried about something, is to talk about it with someone you trust.

Parents and teachers work together with a doctor to decide if ADHD is the cause. If so, they work out a plan. The plan may include working with a special teacher, getting extra help, or taking medicine.

Teachers or **psychologists** often help to decide if a child has ADHD.

ADHD strengths

People with ADHD can be good at many things. They might be full of energy and enjoy having fun. Some other good qualities are listed below.

People with ADHD may be:

- good problem-solvers
- willing to try new things
- able to see things in new and interesting ways.

There is no **cure** for ADHD. Many teenagers and adults have it, too. As children grow older they can learn to use their good abilities and to manage any difficulties they might have.

Many children with ADHD go on to college and university.

Living with ADHD

It is important to be able to concentrate in school.

Children with ADHD may find school difficult. In school, teachers often need pupils to pay attention, sit still, and listen carefully. These kinds of **behaviours** are hard for children with ADHD.

Some children with ADHD find they can work better if they have some extra help in school. They may work with special teachers or assistants who help them to **concentrate** and complete their work.

Special teachers can provide extra help for children with ADHD.

Some people with ADHD find that keeping a list is a good way to remember things. Of course, no two people are alike. Everyone needs to find out what works best for him or her.

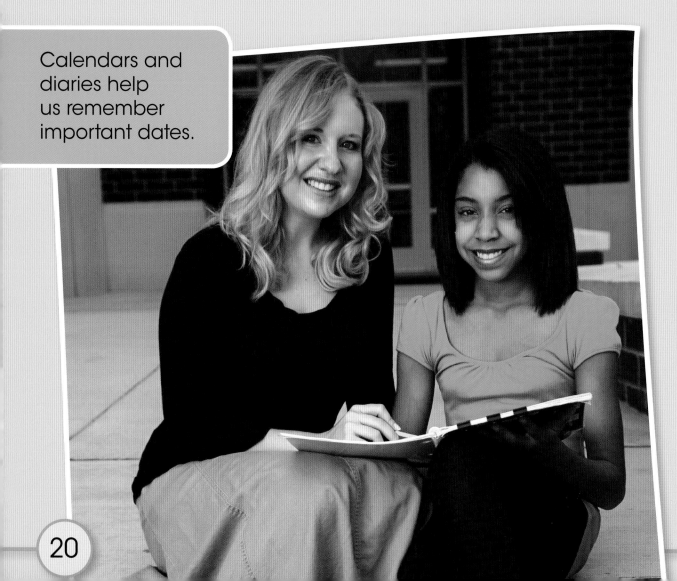

Calendars and diaries help us remember important dates.

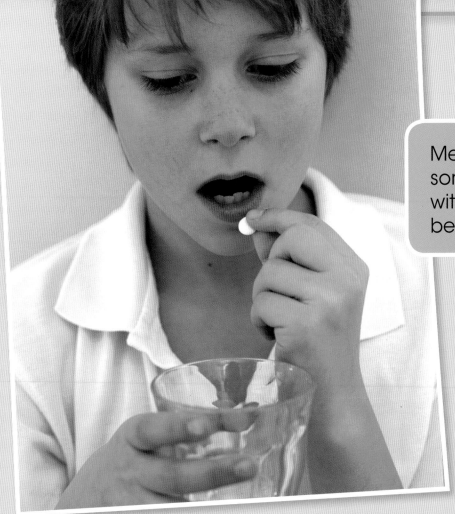

Medicine helps some children with ADHD to do better in school.

Sometimes doctors give children with ADHD medicine to help them **concentrate**. Medicine may also help them to control being **impulsive** or **hyperactive**. However, medicine is not right for everyone.

Being a good friend

Everyone needs a friend. A good friend values the things we do well. A good friend understands when we have problems and tries to help.

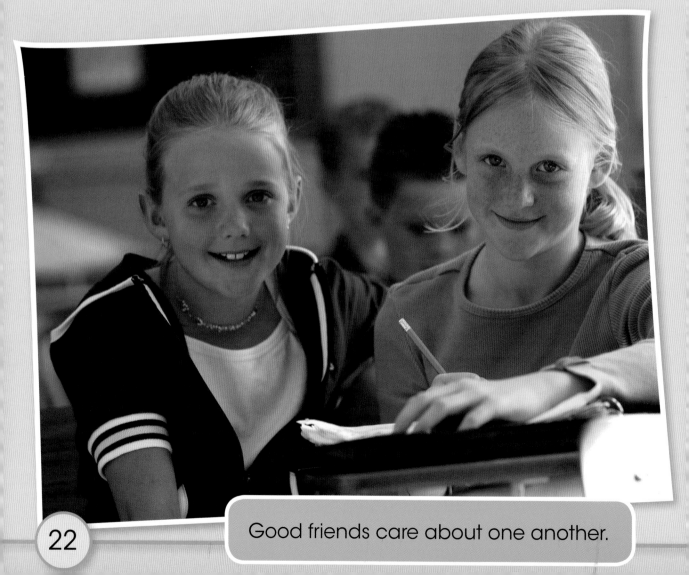

Good friends care about one another.

Friends make life better.

It is important to understand why people with ADHD might behave in certain ways, and to help other people to understand, too. The differences between us help to make life interesting.

Ways to help

There are many ways you can help a friend with ADHD. Try not to **distract** your friend during class. Most of us find it easier to **concentrate** when it is quiet. This can be even more important for someone with ADHD.

Whispering makes it hard to concentrate on what the teacher is saying.

A good group works together to complete a project.

If you are working on a group project, find ways to help everyone do well. Break the project down into smaller jobs. Make sure everyone in the group understands what to do and when to do it.

Famous people

Children with ADHD often become successful adults. They find new ways of solving problems. They aren't afraid to try new things.

US swimming champion Michael Phelps has ADHD.

Michael Phelps won eight gold medals in the 2008 Olympics.

Swimmer Michael Phelps learned that he had ADHD when he was nine. He took medicine to help him succeed in school. Michael Phelps has become a world-champion swimmer.

ADHD – true or false?

Children with ADHD can be as clever as anyone else.

TRUE! Children with ADHD can be clever, creative, and good problem solvers – just like anyone else.

You can catch ADHD from someone who has it.

FALSE! It is not possible to catch ADHD.

For every twenty children around the world, one is likely to have ADHD.

TRUE! There is a good chance that someone in your class might have ADHD.

Glossary

behaviour way of acting

chemicals the materials that make up the world around us. Some chemicals, such as lead, cause problems if they are taken into the body.

concentrate give all your attention to something

cure medical treatment that makes someone better

distract disturb or draw attention away from something else

fidget move around restlessly

hyperactive restless, always moving and unable to sit still for long periods

impulsive likely to act quickly without thought

psychologist person trained to treat people with ADHD and other learning or behaviour difficulties

Find out more

Books to read

How to Deal with ADHD, Lynette Robbins
  (PowerKids Press, 2010)

My Friend has ADHD, Amanda Doering Tourville
  (Picture Window Books, 2010)

Websites

kidshealth.org/kid
Visit Kids Health and enter ADHD in the 'Search here' box to learn more.

www.fffbi.com/info/academy.html
This site has games designed for children with ADHD.

Index